THE Magic OF Friends

Written and Compiled by Laurie Kay

In writing this book, I traveled the country and people from many walks of life shared with me things they remembered their fathers doing for them as children that made them feel special. These shared memories are important to all of us because they remind us that in any language and in any culture, even the simplest things we say or do can have a powerful and lasting impact on the lives of others.

I hope you will find inspiration in this book and discover some of your own memories to share with your friends. These memories really do reveal the magic that is... The Magic of Friends.

This book is dedicated
to my *Friends*

As friends we are so close, like sisters, that we fondly refer to ourselves as the "Triplets." Over the past ten years we've supported each other through happy times, family turmoil, serious illness, divorce, marriage, birth, and through the process of our children growing up, graduating, leaving home, and getting married. We even took a "girl's cruise" together just to relax, laugh, and have fun. Although we don't see each other often, every time we get together, we just pick up where we left off, get caught up on each other's lives and continue our "sisterhood."

- "The Triplets" (Robyn, Linda and Laurie)

I have found the best in many of my friends.

Each has a unique gift to share with me — to listen... to make

me laugh... to do things with me... to just talk.

I value each of these friendships and

cherish the joy they bring.

- Ruth

After smoking for twenty-one years, I finally

made the tough decision to quit. My friend stuck

with me and supported and

encouraged me during the

entire process. I've not had a cigarette in twelve years

and I thank her for helping me through it.

She helped save my life.

- Adrian

I have a dear friend who shares my love for movies.

We call each other and decide which movie to see,

then meet at the theater, enjoy a good movie, and

afterwards eat a bite at a nearby sandwich shop.

All in all, it turns out to be *a very*

good adventure

for a couple of good friends.

- Pat

I am thankful for my girlfriend. She is someone I can trust and who can make me feel better when it seems that life is just too much to handle!

- Bonnie

My friend and I have a special friendship.

The laughter, the tears, the phone calls, the emails,

the shopping, the movies, the lunches, the dinners,

the late night talks. These are the things that

comprise the special bond

that's unique to us.

- Shirley

After my wedding day, my best friend presented me with *a special gift.* She had thoughtfully planted the ivy from my bridal bouquet in a beautiful pot for me to keep for many years as a memento of my wedding day.

- Bethany

My best friend and I grew up together and have

been through a lot together. I am completely

comfortable around her and she would

do anything for me. If I don't

see her for a long time, it's always okay because

we just pick up where we left off.

- Marg

A very dear friend of mine *made me feel special* when she told me, "You are a wonderful, caring person and people who know you can see your heart through your eyes."

- Janice

Where I worked, a group of us made time in our busy schedules to get together once a week to talk on a spiritual basis. We always chose an inspirational book to read and use as the basis of our discussions. We called our little group the "MOM" group (it stood for Meeting of the Minds). We grew close together as a result of our ongoing discussions and we all agreed that we benefited from having "soul sister" friends to meet our spiritual need.

- Laurel

Through his *forthrightness and honesty* my friend has enabled me to see myself in a true light.

- Pat

My friend has been *there for me* when I thought no one else was and with her honesty she made me face reality when I didn't want to. She can get through to me because she knows just what to say and how to say it.

- Victoria

I helped a friend get settled into her new office.

As a token of her appreciation, she gave me a beau-

tiful African violet plant that produced a multitude

of deep purple blossoms. My friend later moved

on, but the plant flourished and every time it burst

into purple bloom, it reminded me of her and

her kindness.

- Sharon

I have a group of friends that are like sisters to me.

They've been supportive when I've struggled with

financial and marital difficulties. When things get

tough, they *encourage me* and

do whatever it takes to help me get through it.

- Marie

I have a good friend who is special because she

and I can just be silly together. Basically,

she accepts me for who

I am and doesn't try to change me.

- Judy

The best thing about my friend is that if one of

us is having a difficult time, all we have to do is

pick up the phone and the other one is

there to listen.

- Susanne

I went through a very difficult divorce and through

this trying time, I had a group of friends who

lent me an ear... *offered a*

shoulder to cry on... and later shared

in my joys. Through their actions, these friends

taught me the true meaning of friendship and

helped me see how I can be a true friend to others.

- Roberta

My best friend and I don't take ourselves too seriously and we accept each other's faults and differences. These characteristics of a friendship have created a **strong bond between us.**

- Gayle

*A*t one point in time I lost touch with my closest friend

— whom I'd known for many, many years

— but we were able to find each other again through

the internet. Once we re-established our friendship, she

invited me to move closer to her and her family; so I did.

I've been blessed with this once-in-a-lifetime friend —

there isn't anything she wouldn't do for me. Having her

as a friend has changed my life... my life would not

be what it is today without her.

- Patty

My best friend

always keeps me from making a

complete fool of myself.

Enough said.

- Mike

My most special friends are those who

accept me for who I

am — not for how I look or for what I have.

For me that's the true meaning of friendship.

- Corinne

I have a friend who is special because

when she receives a gift of food from someone,

she always returns the dish with something

else in it. That small gesture is a sign of

her overall generosity
toward others.

- Danielle

I have learned that people make mistakes (me included!). **Through my friends,** I have learned to shrug my shoulders and accept that I am only human and can't be perfect.

- Rosalie

I have a friend who has shown me that it is okay

for men to be honest and truthful, supportive and

understanding
as friends.

- Jacob

I have a friend who is  *very special*

because she is there when I need to talk and she

knows more about me than I know myself.

- Judith

I have a special friend who is a *real* *inspiration* to me. She is blind but doesn't let her physical limitation keep her from trying things and doing as much as she can for herself. Her perseverance amazes me and is driven by her attitude that, if you think you're beaten, you are.

- Belinda

I have a friend that stands out from any other.

Through her *encouragement and support,* she helped me

get through the loss of my son. She is very

intuitive and has the unique ability to pick

me up when I am down.

- Donna

When I learned that I had a serious health problem and was instructed by my doctor to walk on a daily basis, my friend quietly supported me by being outside my door every morning to meet me sans makeup, hair pulled back, and with her gym shoes on... ready to go.

- Linda

The thing that is so special about my closest friend is that she's *willing to help* me with anything — anything at all. She gives unselfishly and doesn't expect anything in return.

- Nancy

After the death of my mother, my friend came over
just to "be" with me.
It was very comforting to have a friend like that.

- Cheryl

My dearest friend helps me so much through my struggles. She quiets my fears and *raises my spirits* — especially when she reminds me that I can always choose between faith and fear.

- Jeannette

As a young man, I taunted and picked on

a guy twice my size. He later became my best

friend and could "put me in my place" when I

needed it. We now share a mutual respect for

each other and I have *great*

admiration for him.

-Fred

My friend and I both travel a lot, but she

makes me feel special because she calls

just to say "Hi" and *keeps in*

touch with me on a regular basis.

- Jan

My friend and I can talk about anything,

share the joys and
problems in our lives, and

laugh and cry together. I know she will

always be there for me.

- Marla

I have a friend who is like a brother to me. We are similar in many ways and have the unique ability to communicate on a gut level. As a good friend, he calls me on my stuff, snaps me back to reality, and helps me deal with life on life's terms — not mine. He's the one I will pick up the phone and call for anything. We *care about each other* and are there for whatever the need — that's what friendship is all about.

- Larry

A friend of mine has a physical handicap, but does not

let that stop her from doing most anything that anyone

else can do. Instead of feeling sorry for herself, she

reaches out to others

and is the best friend one could ask for.

- Jennifer

Our family didn't have much money when I was growing up, but because of our mother's great love for us, we felt rich and didn't know we were poor. In much the same way, I have a friend that makes me feel rich because she takes time to care and show a special interest in me.

- Fran

Of all my friends, the **most** *special friend* is the one who understands me and values and appreciates me for who I am.

- Francine

I have a special friend who with her

humor and cheer-
fulness *always picks me up.*

One can't help but be happy around her.

- Sandra

When my dog died after being with me

for nine years, my best friend came over and

just hung out with me for awhile. I know he

did it because he *understood*

what I was going

through at that time.

- Russell

In high school I had a friend who was like a brother to me. He taught me about cars, geometry, and life in general. No matter what I needed to talk about, he was there to listen, support, encourage and never judge. I sought him out and he was there to listen even when I had problems that I couldn't tell my parents. He was a special friend.

- Laurel

My friend and I have shared good times

and bad times, laughter and tears, guiding and

helping each other

through the hard times.

- Jessica

My boss is also a good friend who

doesn't give up

on me, forgives my mistakes, and

is always encouraging me.

- Mitchell

Our family had dear friends who lived on a farm in another state. Some summers we would stop by to visit them as we drove to our vacation destination. They didn't have much, but this special couple would always greet us upon our arrival and offer us a welcome gift. Often it was something they had made or fresh produce from their garden. I remember these *simple gifts* as being the best welcome gifts we ever received from anyone.

They were truly gifts from the heart.

- Chris

A friend of my father's had an old car that I thought was great. When I turned sixteen and got my driver's license, my father's friend challenged me to a friendly game of pool. I won, and unbeknownst to me the prize he gave me for winning was his car! That was my first car and I drove it for many years.

P.S. I'm sure that as a true family friend, he **let me win** that game of pool.

- Richard

I have a friend who is one of a kind.

She is a kindred spirit. Her friendship is unique

because we can talk about anything or say anything

and we don't judge each other. Our

friendship is solid because it is based on

unconditional love. We will be friends forever.

- Birgitta

My friend accepts me as I am, *believes*
in me and never judges me.

- Lynn

My friend is the best partner for talking,

talking, talking... and listening,
listening, listening.

- Darlene

My best friend is my best friend because she would

do **anything** for me.

- Cassandra

My friend and I have been through a lot together.

She helped me through my divorce. We have cried

together and laughed together, but most of all we

have been there for
each other when we felt alone.

- Anna

My best friend is always available to

shop, share, heal, joke, or *just be with me.*

- Mary

My best friend  makes me feel special because she listens without judging.

- Janelle

A special friend and I saw an old ceramic child's cereal bowl at a yard sale. The bowl was unique and interesting to us—and it was only fifty cents, but the glaze was cracked and the design faded. Not being experts in the field of antiques, we decided not to buy it. An hour later, we were at an antique shop in town where we saw an identical bowl for fifty dollars! As we quickly returned to the yard sale hoping to purchase the antique bowl we saw, my friend said, "If the bowl is still there I want you to have it." Then she handed me the money

to buy it. I could not believe her unselfishness! Not only

was she offering to let me have the antique bowl, but

she was giving me the money to buy it as well! As it

turned out, the bowl was gone, but I was quite touched

by the poignant lesson learned from my
friend's generosity.

- Laurel

*If this book has touched you and you would like to share
with us a memory of your own, please email us at*
memory@magicof.com

© 2005 Havoc Publishing
San Diego, California
U.S.A.

Text by Laurie Kay

ISBN 0-7416-1324-7

www.havocpub.com

Made in China